tales of
Willow View

Kerralye Wright

First published by Ultimate World Publishing 2024
Copyright © 2024 Kerralye Wright

ISBN
Hardback: 978-1-923255-15-9
Ebook: 978-1-923255-16-6

Kerralye Wright has asserted her rights under the Copyright, Designs and Patents Act 1988 to be identified as the author of this work. The information in this book is based on the author's experiences and opinions. The publisher specifically disclaims responsibility for any adverse consequences which may result from use of the information contained herein. Permission to use information has been sought by the author. Any breaches will be rectified in further editions of the book.

All rights reserved. No part of this publication may be reproduced, stored in or introduced into a retrieval system, or transmitted in any form, or by any means (electronic, mechanical, photocopying, recording or otherwise) without the prior written permission of the author. Any person who does any unauthorised act in relation to this publication may be liable to criminal prosecution and civil claims for damages. Enquiries should be made through the publisher.

Cover design: Ultimate World Publishing
Layout and typesetting: Ultimate World Publishing
Artwork by: Kerralye Wright
Editor: Victoria Pickens

Ultimate World Publishing
Diamond Creek,
Victoria Australia 3089
www.writeabook.com.au

Dedication

In loving memory of my cherished grandparents, whose presence continues to illuminate my path. This book is dedicated to my dearest grandma, whose boundless love and timeless wisdom will forever stay close to my heart.

Acknowledgement of Country

I acknowledge and pay respects to the Traditional Owners of the Land. I pay my respects to their Elders past, present, and emerging.

Contents

Dedication	3
Acknowledgement of Country	3
The Bull	6
Birly	8
Cooking	12
The Sponge Cake	14
The Original Recipe	16
Washing Day	18
The Seamstress	20
School Days	22
The Switchboard	26
The White Sheet	28
Milking	30
The Gold Locket	34
About Me	37
About the Author	39

The Bull

In the late 1940s grandma and pop married in a humble setting at grandma's parents' farm. After a few years working on various small local farms, ranging from pineapple plantations to pig and dairy farms, they saved enough money to buy a farm of their own on the Brisbane River naming it 'Willow View'.

Their new farm became a bustling sanctuary, complete with cows, pigs, cattle dogs, chooks, and vigilant geese. In particular, the geese served as diligent guards, alerting everyone with loud honking and frenzied flapping at any sign of trouble. With a large property and all the animals to tend to, coupled with the responsibilities of raising three boys, my grandparents days were filled with relentless activity.

Twice daily, without fail, they embarked on the task of milking the cows, once at dawn and again at dusk. However, despite their industriousness, challenges loomed on the horizon. At the age of 40, pop's health took a turn for the worse with a diagnosis of arthritis, casting a shadow over their idyllic farm life.

In a happy turn of events, just before his diagnosis, the family attended the local royal show where he encountered a magnificent bull that captured his heart. Consumed by admiration, he couldn't stop talking about it. As the show drew to a close, he made the decision to purchase the bull, with the thought the bull's bloodline would improve his herd. Pop made the journey to Biloela to pick up his prized purchase. Naming the bull 'Tribladore'. Pop's pride swelled as he welcomed this majestic creature to their farm, heralding a new chapter in their agricultural endeavours.

Reminiscing discussion questions:
Have you ever lived on a farm?
Do you love looking at a country scene, or do you prefer the beach, or a city view?
Name some animals you might find on the farm?

Birly

Pop and grandma were known in the local community for their generosity towards the lads from the local boys' home, offering them both work and lodging. The lodgings were located underneath the house, a space typically reserved for grandma's prized preserved fruit collection. However, there was one lad among them who had a perpetual hunger, unbeknownst to grandma. He stealthily indulged in the preserved fruit, consuming half of it and then diluting the remainder with water before sealing the jars. When grandma eventually discovered the jars, the fruit had become mouldy, and was inedible. Needless to say, grandma no longer stored the fruit where the boys could find it.

Among the boys was another lad named Birly who had many talents. He entertained the household with his guitar-strumming renditions of songs by Chubby Checker. Yet, Birly's contributions weren't solely musical; he possessed a deep understanding of the land. Grandma often mentioned how eager Birly was to share his knowledge, spending every spare moment with her three boys. Looking back on Birly's time on the farm, my dad affectionately noted, "Birly was such a fun companion. He radiated warmth, joy, and a strong work ethic."

Birly's influence extended beyond entertainment and storytelling; he taught the boys practical skills, such as crafting four-prong spears from high tensile wire and bamboo. Together, the boys spent countless hours honing their spear-making skills under Birly's watchful eye, before trekking down to the Brisbane River to test their creations and fishing skills. Their efforts often yielded a proud catch, predominantly catfish, which grandma would expertly prepare for supper.

Reminiscing discussion questions:
Do you like fishing?
Where is your favourite fishing spot?
What fish did you catch?
What fruit would you preserve?
Did you have someone like Birly you grew up with?

Cooking

At Willow View farm, the kitchen was always bustling with activity as family and friends often dropped by. Grandma was renowned for her culinary skills, a reputation unanimously upheld by all who tasted her delicious creations. From delectable sponge cakes adorned with mock cream to indulgent lamingtons, creamy baked custard, comforting bread and butter pudding, savoury and sweet pies, homemade ice cream, and fluffy pumpkin scones. Grandma's repertoire knew no bounds. Despite the modest setting of the farmhouse kitchen—comprising a simple table, bench, sink, and wood stove—it was the heart of the home, where warmth and laughter filled the air.

Reflecting on the bygone era of the 1950s and 1960s, life seemed remarkably simpler. Despite the advent of countless time-saving inventions in both the kitchen and laundry, the essence of those times remains cherished. In the kitchen, the cook would deftly stir and beat mixtures with a humble wooden spoon, with the introduction of the whisk marking an exciting advancement. The invention of the electric beater revolutionised households, offering newfound convenience. Today, many kitchens boast the presence of a Thermomix, a modern marvel capable of effortlessly blending and mixing ingredients. Yet, amidst the technological advancements, there's a nostalgic charm in the simplicity and tradition of the past that continues to resonate with many.

Reminiscing discussion questions:
How does grandma's kitchen compare to your own memories, or experiences of family gatherings and shared meals?
Consider the technology advancements mentioned in the story. How have these changed how we cook today?
What was your favourite recipe to cook?

The Sponge Cake

Grandma's specialty was her sponge cake, a delicacy that I can still recall: the softness, fluffiness, and the lightness of each bite. One unforgettable memory stands out: the day grandma visited me and together we cooked her sponge cake. It was astonishing to witness how effortlessly she recited the recipe from memory.

Mock cream, not used as much now days, held a special place in grandma's heart. She took great delight in whipping up this creamy, buttery delight. Truly, a culinary experience to remember.

Recipe reflection:
What recipe do you know off by heart?
Have you tasted mock cream?
Can you name your favourite cake?

THE ORIGINAL RECIPE

W. M. U. Cookery Book 1961

SPONGE CAKE

4 eggs
1 level cup sugar
1 cup plain flour
1 teaspoon corn flour
1 tablespoon butter
4 tablespoons hot water
1 teaspoon cream of tartare
½ teaspoon carbonate soda.

METHOD

Beat whites and yolks of eggs separately, add sugar to whites gradually, then add yolks. Sift flour, corn flour and cream of tartar (3 times). Fold into eggs. Add soda to boiling butter and water and mix into sponge lightly. Bake in slow oven about 20 minutes.

MOCK CREAM

¼ pound butter and ¾ sugar, beat together and keep adding a little hot water until sugar dissolves (castor sugar may be better).

Washing Day

When our babies were born, grandma would come and stay to help us out. I remember a day when she was helping me with the never-ending laundry pile, and she remarked on how washing had evolved over the years. She reminisced about her days on the farm and how laundry was done back then.

In the days before electricity, grandma would begin by kindling a fire in the stove. Then, she would fill a large copper tub with water and stir in the clothes and detergent (in a little blue bag) with a wooden paddle. The clothes would simmer in the water for at least thirty minutes. Grandma had to keep an eye on the tub stirring every so often so the clothes didn't stick together. Once the boiling process had finished, grandma would carefully transfer the heavy tub, laden with hot water and clothes, to the bench to cool. After rinsing and wringing out the clothes, they were ready to be hung out to dry.

Grandma reflected on the day she brought home her electric wringer washer or mangle washer. No more lifting the heavy copper pot off the stove. The wringer washer had a similar washing procedure but with added conveniences like a rinse cycle and a wringer to extract excess water from the clothes. Grandma's strength from years of manually wringing out washing was evident; she often proved it by twisting an apple in half with her hands, a testament to her remarkable strength.

Reminiscing reflection:
How did your mother wash the clothes?
Have you seen a wringer washer before?
Do you think the advancement of technology has impacted our daily lives? Why?

The Seamstress

From the young age of 14, grandma immersed herself in the world of sewing, displaying such great ability that she ended up sewing clothes for the whole family. With skills that spanned from sewing, knitting, crocheting, embroidery, and meticulous mending, she embodied the essence of a perfectionist. During her sewing lessons with me over the years, she imparted invaluable wisdom, emphasising the importance of embracing unpicking as an integral part of the learning process and the journey toward creating masterpieces you could be proud of. Grandma often said, "You don't want the finished product to look homemade." Every seam was carefully overlocked and hidden.

Grandma's repertoire of creations knew no bounds. From tailoring her own wedding dress to clothing for herself, her family, and later, maternity dresses adorned with delicate smocking for her granddaughters and great-granddaughters, she demonstrated remarkable skilfulness and creativity. Armed with nothing but her natural talent, grandma tackled her sewing projects without the aid of patterns. Instead, she sketched her designs and drafted her patterns onto paper.

A touching testament to grandma's skill and devotion to her craft is evident in the bridesmaid dresses she tailored for my wedding. Guided by a simple sketch I drew on a scrap of paper with measurements and fabric sent via the post. Grandma began the mammoth task of sewing five bridesmaid dresses with unwavering determination. Upon their completion, she flew to Adelaide with the dresses neatly packed in her suitcase. To my astonishment and delight, the dresses perfectly mirrored my vision, each one a stunning reflection of grandma's talent. Without the need for any adjustments, the dresses fitted my five bridesmaids perfectly, a true testament to grandma's skill and unwavering commitment to perfectionism.

Reminiscing questions:
What types of fabrics do you like to touch?
Can you sketch a dress?
What was your special talent? e.g., drawing, sewing, painting, building, singing, or playing an instrument.

School Days

I loved listening to my grandma's stories from her youth. One day she recounted how she used to travel to school on a horse with her sister, a tradition that continued with her own boys. The idea of riding a horse to school sounds thrilling to me. Grandma shared memories of riding bareback with her sister, both perched atop their horse named 'Trixie'. When her boys attended school, they were fortunate enough to each have their own horse. My dad's horse was named 'Velvet'.

I asked my dad about his school days, and the first thing he mentioned was how frequently "us boys were getting the cane". He recalled a time when classrooms were characterised by strict discipline and order, a far cry from the classroom atmosphere today. In those days, students typically attended school up to grade seven or eight. This was common for children born in farm families, where education often took a back seat.

Reminiscing reflection:
Where did you attend school?
What was your favourite subject in school?
What is your favourite school memory?
Working your way through the alphabet, can you take turns in saying boys' names starting with the letter 'A'?

The Switchboard

When telephones were first invented, calls had to be routed through switchboards, connecting callers with one another. My grandma often reminisced about the days when the switchboard operator played a pivotal role, not only in connecting calls but also in eavesdropping on conversations. The switchboard operator was the unofficial gossiper, she was privy to every juicy detail circulating through the community.

One day, my grandma made a call and, out of curiosity or perhaps intuition, the switchboard operator chose to stay on the line. Little did we know; this decision would soon prove to be lifesaving. Here's how the story unfolds:

My uncle, then just a baby learning to roll around, had an insatiable love for his milk bottle and found himself in a precarious situation. During his innocent exploration, he accidently knocked a bottle of kerosene off a shelf and began ingesting its contents. By the time grandma found him, he had swallowed a distressing amount of kerosene, with the smell of it heavy on his breath. In a panic, my grandma rushed to the telephone, urgently asking the switchboard operator to connect her with her sister (who lived on a nearby farm). Sensing the urgency in my grandma's voice, the operator remained on the line to listen. Without hesitation, the operator quickly called through to the ambulance service on my grandma's behalf.

Thanks to the meddling operator help arrived quickly. Upon examination, it became apparent that my uncle's love of milk had inadvertently saved his life. The milk coating his stomach and oesophagus prevented the kerosene from causing permanent damage. Also, my grandma's frantic sprint to inform my pop in the milking shed inadvertently aided my uncle's recovery by facilitating air circulation in his lungs.

This remarkable chain of events, from the switchboard operator's keen intuition (or nosiness) to the milk lining my uncle's airways, ensured that what could have been a tragedy turned into a tale of survival.

Reminiscing reflection:
Where were you born?
What are the names of your siblings?
Is there anything you would like to share about your life story or experiences?
Thinking about how much telephones have changed do you remember your first telephone?

The White Sheet

Can you imagine a time without phones or radio transmitters? It's a notion I find hard to entertain!

My grandma once shared with me the challenge of gathering everyone for meals on the farm. She came up with a brilliant idea: hanging a white sheet over the veranda railing. Positioned high on the house, the veranda was visible from nearly every corner of the farm. Grandma recounted how, with ravenous boys and busy workers, the sight of the white sheet became a beacon, signalling a welcome respite for the weary labourers. Especially on days when the sun was scorching and the humidity was high, a cool drink and a moment of shade were eagerly anticipated by all.

For grandma, the hanging of the white sheet served as a clever tactic to entice the boys back home for meals or to begin their daily chores.

Reminiscing reflection:
Throughout history, people have employed various means of communication to exchange information. Can you name some? I can think of at least ten.
What did the first phone you used look like? Let's look up some pictures.

Milking

On a farm, there is a never-ending list of chores that demand attention and diligence. In addition to milking the cows and tending to their feed, water, and health needs, my grandparents had to do many other jobs to ensure the smooth operation of their farm. These included repairs and maintenance of farming equipment, record-keeping, pest management, gardening, watering, spraying the pests, worming and marking all the animals. Farming is a combination of hard work, dedication, and expertise. My grandma would remark, "Your pop and I never felt like there were enough hours in the day to get all the work done."

Pop and grandma had 130 milking cows on their farm that they milked twice daily using a milking machine. In those days the milk was accomplished with a separator, with only the cream being sold. In her younger days, grandma recalled loading the cream onto a horse-drawn cart for transport into town. As she later managed the farm with pop, daily cream collection occurred conveniently at the front of their property. It was common practice among farmers of that era to forego consumption of the milk product, instead opting to sell the cream while using the remainder to feed the pigs and calves, helping them to be fat and healthy.

Reminiscing reflection:
Reflecting on farm duties, can you think of any?
How many types of farms can you think of? I can think of at least ten.
Do you have any farming experience?
Can you name some animals you might see on a hobby farm?

The Gold Locket

For as long as I can remember grandma wore a large gold locket hanging from her necklace. If I asked to look inside, with pride she'd open it, with trembling hands overwhelmed by emotion revealing tiny black and white profile photos of her boys.

Throughout her lifetime grandma faced numerous hardships. Regrettably, grief became part of her journey. It's often said that 'no parent should have to bury their children', yet sadly, grandma experienced this heartache twice in her lifetime burying two of her sons. Additionally, my pop's life was cut short when he sadly passed away in his early 50s.

My grandparent's youngest son (my uncle) passed away tragically in a farming accident just before his 14th birthday. The story goes like this; my uncle had woken up in the morning telling grandma he felt sick, so she allowed him to stay home from school. While they were out picking up some necessities from town, he was busy finishing off his Sunday School homework, as this was the agreement, he could stay home from school if he finished his homework. He carefully laid his homework out on his bed ready to show grandma when she returned, he then drove the tractor down to the front of the property which is something he had done many times before. A fortnight before he had been banned from the tractor for driving onto the neighbour's property and also for driving recklessly. Unfortunately, his love for speed and recklessness led to a fatal accident when, coming down the hill, he rolled the tractor. This tragedy left a profound impact on the family. It was hard for the

Reminiscing reflection:
Reflect on your own experiences with grief and loss.
How does grandma's approach to coping with grief resonate with you?
Do you have a story you would like to share about losing a loved one?

family to recover from this accident, and it wasn't long before pop's health declined dramatically. To help ease the burden of finances and farm work my grandparents built a small house at the front of the farm for share farmers to live-in. Eventually when it all became too much and pop's health had rapidly declined, they sold the farm and moved to Brisbane, settling in a seaside town, they were both seeking some much-needed rest.

Although grief is a topic often avoided, I believe it can hold significant importance in our lives, it certainly did in grandma's. Reflecting and reminiscing about her boys especially, in her old age the passing of her boys and pop became a topic she often discussed. Grandma's love for babies and children was evident, she would always offer a compassionate and understanding ear to grieving parents who had also lost their children or joyfully knit garments for newborns. I often took grandma down to the beach for an outing in her wheelchair. One day as we were walking along the waterfront, we stopped to listen to a busker singing "Fernando" by ABBA. After a while, a little girl came up and started dancing to the music. It was a joy to watch grandma clapping and laughing cupping her face with delight. The little girl must have sensed grandma's joy because she stopped at one point, came up, and held grandma's hand. Tears streamed down grandma's face, it was such a touching moment. Witnessing grandma's adoration for children was truly a beautiful experience.

A close friend once told me when discussing the topic of grief: "Time doesn't heal the pain for a parent who has lost a child, instead: with time comes the strength to face the world with a brave heart."

Reminiscing reflection:
Isn't it a joy watching children laugh and play?
Can you share any stories that highlight your values, beliefs, or life philosophy?

About Me

My name is Kerralye Wright, and I am blessed to be married to my childhood sweetheart. Together, we have three wonderful sons who bring joy and adventure into our lives. As you read this book, I hope you can sense the deep love and adoration I have for my grandparents, especially my grandma.

Over the years, my passion for listening to the stories of the elderly has blossomed, particularly through my work in Aged Care. Each person I encounter has a unique and rich life story to tell, full of wisdom, experiences, and lessons learned. This book is a tribute to those stories and a gentle reminder to cherish the moments spent with your parents or grandparents. Take the time to listen to them reflect on their lives and the journeys they've undertaken.

My hope is that this book will not only inspire you, but also provide you with the tools to engage in meaningful conversations with your loved ones. Reflecting on their life stories can bring you closer and offer invaluable insights into their world. May this book serve as a bridge to deeper connections and cherished memories with those you hold dear.

About the Author

Following her grandma's dementia diagnosis, Kerralye began looking for a calming and engaging book to read to her grandma. After much searching Kerralye soon discovered that many stories were either too complex or lengthy for her grandma's needs.

Determined to provide her grandma with engaging stories, Kerralye decided to write down the stories her grandma often told. Her goal was to compile these stories into a book tailored specifically for individuals with a short attention span, offering them moments of meaningful connections.

Kerralye's grandma sadly passed away before she could complete the project. Nonetheless, Kerralye's efforts aim to honour her grandma's memory and provide comfort and stimulation to others facing similar challenges.

Note from the author:
In telling my grandma's story I have portrayed events as I remember them. I do not claim to present an exact rendition, rather this is solely my perspective on her life.

www.ingramcontent.com/pod-product-compliance
Lightning Source LLC
Chambersburg PA
CBHW042328280426
43661CB00099B/1293